TESTIMONIA

"Alejandro Dabdoub is an extraordinary businessman with a diverse perspective in his field. His years of experience make him an invaluable resource for anyone interested in investing wisely. Having known Alejandro my entire life, I'm well acquainted with his successes in bringing foreign investors into the United States. I admire his ability to commit and care for what he values."

—*Samantha Bopp*
Congressional Staff

"Alejandro Dabdoub's book, *Winning: The Art of Becoming an American Investor*, should be required reading for anyone thinking about investment opportunities in the United States. Mr. Dabdoub has acquired his knowledge from years of experience in the field, and coupled with his hard work and ethics, he is someone to be looked to for advice."

—*Tim L. Myers*
Chairman of the Advisory Board and
Cofounder of Allied Orion Group

"Alejandro Dabdoub is a brilliant investor. If you are a foreign national looking to invest in the United States, his new book, *Winning: The Art of Becoming an American Investor*, is a must-read. This book is full of content you would be hard-pressed to find collected anywhere else."

—*Raymond Aaron*
New York Times Bestselling Author

"Alejandro Dabdoub has written a must-read primer for anyone considering investing in America… Read this book—and learn from one of the best, since Alejandro has spent most of his life studying the intricacies of the financial world."

"Alejandro Dabdoub is first and foremost a great person who has constantly developed throughout his life as a successful businessman. Visionary, analytical, prudent and courageous, among many other attributes. I have maintained a great friendship with Alejandro for over a decade, and I certainly believe that his contribution to the business world interested in investing in the USA will be invaluable. His work is original and shares much of the experience that Alejandro has cultivated for years."

"Thrilled to see Alejandro sharing his treasure trove of experiences and knowledge with the foreign national investment community in this very worthwhile read. He has for over 20 years been a trusted resource for me and for the many who I've pointed in his direction. Alejandro combines a genuine desire to be of service with proven formulas to achieve maximum investment returns in this publication."

"I've known Alejandro Dabdoub for more than 20 years. He's bi-cultural, successful in international business, has a sound work ethic and when he tells you he'll do something, it will get done. I wholeheartedly recommend him."

—Emilio "Millo" Aragon
Investor Relations Manager

Winning

THE ART OF BECOMING
AN AMERICAN INVESTOR

Alejandro Dabdoub Smutny

10-10-10
Publishing

WINNING: The Art of Becoming an American Investor

BecomingAnAmericanInvestor.com

bookofinvesting@gmail.com

Publisher
10-10-10 Publishing
Markham, ON
Canada

Printed in Canada and the United States of America

CONTENTS

ACKNOWLEDGEMENTS

I want to acknowledge and thank the following people:

My father, who was also my mentor, always guided and inspired me to be the person I am today. Although sometimes rough in his teachings, he knew which buttons to push to make me better and encourage me to pursue my dreams—no matter what people thought or how impossible those dreams seemed to be.

My mother taught me how to be ethical and treat people equally, regardless of the situation.

My godparents cared for me for many years and taught me many things about life that I never would have learned while living at home. I am so grateful to have had them as guides and mentors in my life.

My wife inspires me to do the best for her and the kids. With her push as an incentive, I am always willing to try new ventures and explore the world; without her support, I wouldn't be here today writing this book.

FOREWORD

Alejandro Dabdoub Smutny is a partner who epitomizes the phrase *international investor*. Originally from Mexico, Alejandro began investing in the United States at a young age. Parlaying his education and contacts into real-world results, he has built up a portfolio of companies that are the envy of many.

Along the way, Alejandro became an expert in investing in this country, to the point where he and his family became permanent residents in the United States. He now shares that knowledge with foreign clients, helping them to achieve their dreams through investing in this great country, just as he has done.

You would be hard-pressed to find someone more competent to teach you the ropes regarding investing in the US from another country. Put your money to work the smart way and learn the ins and outs of this kind of investing. Pick up emigration tips, look at the legal entities available to you, learn about the various types of investment visas the US has to offer, or roll up your sleeves and dig into investment opportunity analysis. Whatever topic you select from the Table of Contents of this book, Alejandro has real value to offer.

So, if you want to learn how to successfully invest in the US—in good times and in tough times—pick up a copy of *Winning: The Art of becoming an American Investor* today, then give Alejandro a call. You'll be glad you did.

—Loral Langemeier, The Millionaire Maker, is one of today's most visible and innovative money experts. She's a sought after speaker, entrepreneurial thought leader and best-selling author of five books. Loral accelerates the conversation about money, sharing how to not just survive this tough economic climate, but how to succeed and thrive.

INTRODUCTION

Winning: The Art of Becoming an American Investor is a book about chipping off a piece of the American dream for yourself and your family. It's for the international investor who wants to live in the United States and invest in the country.

The book begins by asking you to define the purpose of the investment you're considering, then devising a plan to make it happen. There's also a description of what you need to do, and the actions you need to take, to actually begin investing in the United States. You may be surprised by what you read.

A discussion then takes place regarding the different kinds of visas available and their function as it pertains to investing.

Moving on to company structures, Alejandro Dabdoub Smutny talks confidently about the various entities available to you, as well as the various components of estate planning, so as to keep your hard-earned money from being decimated by relatives and various outside forces.

Next on the roster is a short chapter regarding the power of alliances.

This is followed by a detailed treatise on analyzing companies for the purpose of investing. Some terrific tools are laid out for you, and Alejandro shows you how to use them.

The latter chapters are designed to help you make the transition from your country to the United States—focusing on taxation, banking, due diligence and the like. There's even a questionnaire designed to test your readiness for taking action.

Sprinkled amidst these chapters are a few case studies that give real life examples of individuals and companies that are in investing in the US.

All in all, Alejandro has compiled a fantastic collection of the things you need to know to become a successful foreign investor in the United States.

*S*tart by doing what's necessary; then do what's possible; and suddenly you are doing the impossible.

–Francis of Assisi

CHAPTER 1

The Plan

The United States has the world's largest and most innovative economy, an unmatched rule of law, and a free market that is the envy of the international community. For investors, we are the reserve currency.

–John Delaney

Why do I want to invest in the USA?

Investing in the United States should be an easy decision to make. The country represents a quarter of all global economic activity, and it offers a secure migratory system, legal certainty, great educational opportunities, security for you and your family, a strong and stable economy, terrific governmental support, and robust tax advantages.

However, there's one thing on which you must be clear; in the 50 states of the United States of America, there are different opportunities and challenges—each requiring a unique strategy or plan. In other words, to be able to take advantage of everything United States has to offer, there are certain steps you need to follow. I would begin by asking some fundamental questions... Why do you want to go to the US? Where do you want to go within the 50 states? When do you want to go? How do you want to invest? And what challenges will you face?

One of the most challenging barriers to investing in the United States is that if you don't physically travel to the country and do the research, you're buying blind.

Experts in real estate suggest it takes up to 12 months to find the right property, make an offer, arrange to finance and close the deal. In my opinion, it's essential to plan at least one visit to the US to see the potential property before committing to buy.

In fact, without a team working on your behalf, you're at a considerable disadvantage when trying to enter the United States marketplace. Cross-border investors face a litany of regulatory and bureaucratic hurdles, even using representatives with US citizenship. Deals may involve attaining US bank accounts, building US credit scores, getting a Visa, setting up an entity and much more.

It's crucial for you to know which of these challenges you'll encounter. Unfortunately, in many states real estate agents will be unable to help you. Statistics show that 20 percent of real estate agents have been in the business for less than a year. Even more troubling for you is that the deals most agents have experience with are within states, so it's difficult to find one experienced in cross-border real estate investment. This lack of transparency means more middlemen to ensure the property transfer occurs smoothly and legally, which results in increased fees. Other fees that could be problematic include currency exchange fees, bank transfer fees, attorney fees, investment fees, traditional broker fees and third-party contracts. Thus, it's important the right property be found, so the return on investment (R.O.I.) is worthwhile.

Here's another example… Let's say you want to construct a commercial building in the United States. The T.M.F. Group, a leading provider of critical compliance and administrative services, tells us that…

In New York City, it can take you an average of 89 days to obtain construction permits, and there are 15 separate procedures you'll need to follow. These include submitting zoning diagrams, acquiring sewer connection permits, securing department of transportation work permits and being awarded actual occupancy permits. Many of the procedures have fees that can add up to over USD $6,000, and just getting your electricity turned on can take over 60 days.

In Los Angeles, the process might be quicker—with an average of 68 days for the construction permits, but there are 17 procedures you must complete, and the associated costs can be astronomical (just the building plan check and permit costs over USD $48,000). Connection times are also longer, with water taking up to 42 days and electricity about 134 days.

Obviously, some basic research can save you a lot of time, money and frustration.

You also need to figure out the purpose of your investments. In many cases, investors are looking to have their family in a safe environment away from certain harmful situations. In other instances, they want to grow their businesses and invest with others as a safe haven for their capital. For each one of these cases, you have to apply a different immigration or legal structure. If this isn't planned at the beginning, you can expect to spend more money on lawyers, accountants and advisers. Advance planning really is a must, or you won't be able to take advantage of all the benefits that each structure can provide.

And asking yourself some hard questions is recommended... Do I want to migrate or simply invest? Is the state I'm planning to invest in the best one for what I expect? Does it give me the tax security and governmental support I need?

Many people typically move where they have family or friends, and they come into the country without immigration knowledge as to how to legally be in the United States. They look for a school district that has a good reputation or schools that are available to them. Others just want their family to live in the United States and travel back and forth to the home country for business purposes. In any case, you need to have the right kind of visas to legally be in the United States.

Once you know what you're looking for, you can start building your team:

- **Lawyers** are needed to make sure your immigration status is in compliance with your plan. If you don't have one, you could end up becoming a US tax individual, which means you'll have to pay worldwide income and estate taxes or, on the other hand, be deported. A good lawyer can guide you toward the type of legal structure you need. However, you have to know there are many lawyers in this country who think nothing of taking advantage of people and the system. They sue for any reason, just to see what they can get. If you have the right legal structure, they'll typically look for someone else to take advantage of. In most structures, you can be either active or not active with respect to the management of your investments. The choice should depend on your immigration status and how involved you would like to be in the operation.

- **Accountants** can be good tax advisors who can save you and your heirs a lot of money. For example, the United States requires that when you die, your estate pays an estate tax—which varies depending on the governmental party in power—that has, in some cases, been around 50%. If you plan ahead, you can save your kids and spouse the burden of this tax.

  Most accountants offer different types of service, the most basic one being accounting—something I don't recommend. It's always better to have a tax strategist and estate planner, so you can get the most benefits out of the system.

- **Key alliances** demand that you should always look for a proven track record and real experiences. I mention this because there are different ways to analyze your alliances. The first thing, though, is to realize that when you ask for a track record, anyone can write anything on paper. If possible, visit the companies in question and talk to people to get a feeling of whether or not the company is real. And depending on your type of industry and the state in which you're looking to do business, you should do the proper research in the area. There are many governmental agencies and business associations that can help you and guide you in the right direction. If you find the appropriate consultants, they can guide you in every step of the process, as they typically have the right networking in the right areas. Not only can they guide you in the best direction for your business, but they can also introduce you to people within your area and market.

If you're wanting to emigrate, it's important to understand your timeline and determine a strategic plan for the move. In the United States, if you don't give solid timelines to the companies you talk to, they're liable to just move on. Also, if you want to come in legally, you need to take enough time to do the proper paperwork to get your visas and choose the right legal and tax structures.

Case Study: The American Dream

In 2001, as a component of an entrepreneurial class, I had to take on a project for the semester. I was fortunate enough to have the support of my father and his banking relationships and was able to secure a loan and convert my project into reality. I purchased a piece of land in the United States, right next to a Walmart that was going to open a couple of years after my purchase. I built a company in the state of Louisiana because that's where I knew I could have legal support for the structure. After some time, the same banking relationships guided me to lawyers, accountants and key alliances in companies in the state of Texas, specifically in the apartment construction industry. Before I finished organizing everything in this new structure, there came a day when I was coming into the United States, and an immigration officer suggested changing my migratory status, or I would be in trouble. I was fortunate to have put together a superb team in Texas who helped me in every way when .I had to spend some time in my home country without being able to travel for business for six months. This lesson taught me that if you don't do things right, you can spend a lot on lawyers, as well as in time. In the end, I was lucky enough to be able to get an investor visa and keep going with my businesses. From then until 2017, I always had an E2 visas. Now I have an EB5 visa, which has given permanent residence status in the United States for my family and me.

Back then, I had hired an accountant who just recorded my transactions but didn't help me with any tax advice, which was probably the worst mistake I've made to date. Today, I have a tax advisor, an estate planner, a lawyer, and an immigration lawyer who help me save money rather than spend it.

In 2001, I also started investing in an apartment complex company that was recommended to me. Then, after many projects, I was invited to become a partner in 2016. Since then, we've added two new partners and built an investment fund to be able to integrate the whole company. Today, we buy properties, get permitting, manage construction and oversee the finished buildings. We have also made acquisitions from third parties as well as managing them. In 2017, we made second place on the list of Houston area developers for multi-family units.

When people talk about the American dream, let me tell you it's a reality. You need to have a purpose and a commitment to achieving the highest goal, but with the right team and the right mindset, you can achieve anything you put your mind to. Of course, you have to be open because the way things are done in other countries doesn't always work in this one. Adaptability is important, but everything is set for you to make it. You just need to do things right and have a good strategy.

I hope this book serves you as a guide on how to be able to live a prosperous life in a country that offers the peace of mind every investor would like to have.

Notes

CHAPTER 2

Migrating to the U.S.A.

The team with the best players wins.

–Jack Welch

The pros and cons of becoming a citizen

It's always important to analyze the pros and cons of any situation.

The positives of becoming a US citizen are many. There are specific jobs that are only offered to US citizens. You get a US passport, which lets you travel between 160 countries without the need for a visa. You have the ability to bring your family into the country. And you don't have to renew your green card or your visas. Studies also show that you'll be granted better access to education and jobs just by being a citizen. You might even obtain the right to vote or run for office.

On the negative side, if you're a resident and decide to go back to your home country after being in the US more than 186 days, you may lose your status and all the work you've done to become a resident. If you become a resident but not a citizen, you'll need to renew your green card which typically costs about $450, and you may lose your dual citizenship depending on the treaty the US has with the country you were born in. Also, depending on your country of birth, there might be better tax benefits for residents than citizens. In the worst-case scenario, if you don't take the proper steps to be legally in the United States, you could be deported and lose access to any kind of visa for the next five years.

The importance of having a good immigration status

There are different types of visas that we can classify in two main groups: Immigrant and Non-immigrant.

- **Immigrant** - People who are seeking a permanent solution for taking up residence in the United States and who want to get all the benefits of being a legal resident. The solutions available are the: EB-5 Investor Visa, L-1A and H-1B Employment Visas and US company-sponsored or international company Executive Transfers.

- **Non-Immigrant** - People who are seeking a temporary residence in the US. These types of visas are directly related to work status or active investment. The solutions available are E-2, TN, EB-2, EB-3, etc.

The most popular and secure visas are the EB-5 and E-2 Investor Visas

EB-5 Visa (Immigrant)

The United States EB-5 Visa, known as the employment-based fifth preference category or EB-5 Immigrant Investor Visa Program, was introduced in 1990 by the Immigration Act of 1990. It provides a way for eligible immigrant investors to become lawful permanent residents ("green card" holders) by investing $1,800,000 (since November 21, 2019) in a business start-up in the US that will employ at least ten workers. Immigrant investors using the EB-5 program tend to invest in a targeted employment area (TEA), which can be either a rural area or an area with high unemployment. This lowers the investment threshold they must meet to $900,000. The EB-5 program is intended to do two things: encourage foreign investments and promote economic growth. The EB-5 Immigrant Investor Visa Program is just one of five employment-based (EB) programs in the United States.

You can invest individually or through a larger investor pool of investors via regional centers (RC). These are federally approved third-party intermediaries that bring foreign investors together with developers in need of funding. Note: these intermediaries take a commission and are usually private, for-profit businesses approved by the US Citizenship and Immigration Services (USCIS) —which is part of Homeland Security. By the spring of 2017, there were 883 USCIS-approved Regional Centers granting the majority of EB-5 Visas, making the EB-5 program an important source of capital for both developers and the regional centers. It's worth noting that an EB-5 investment delivered through an RC may create economic activity indirectly, rather than as with a direct investment, where the vehicle must directly employ ten or more US workers.

More on the EB-5 Visas

Immigrant Investor Program. As previously mentioned, the EB-5 Visa and the Immigrant Investor Program were created to stimulate the US economy via job creation and capital by encouraging investment from foreign investors.

Two types of projects are eligible for EB-5 Visas

- **Direct Investment EB-5** – projects where the EB-5 investor invests in his or her own business.

- **Regional Center EB-5 Investments** – projects where the EB-5 investor invests in a project company that's sponsored by a USCIS-approved Regional Center.

The first major difference between the two types of EB-5 investments is that RC investments must be sponsored by a USCIS-approved EB-5 Regional Center. This demands an application filed with USCIS where the RC's job creation strategy, management team and project ideas are analyzed and then authorized. However, RC projects are sometimes pre-approved and designated "Exemplar."

The second notable difference between these two types of EB-5 investments is in the way jobs are created. Both must create at least ten new full-time jobs through their investment. But Direct Investment EB-5 projects are required to create countable salaried positions (must maintain payroll records to prove that the employee was a salaried and qualified US worker, which excludes, for example, persons who hold Non-immigrant Visa status such as H-1B or L-1A Visa status), while Regional Center EB-5 projects can also count indirect employment resulting from the investment in the community where the project is located. This is determined through economic statistical methods and doesn't necessarily require the new commercial enterprise to provide salary and wage records to confirm that it employed a specific number of employees.

E-2 Visas to Treaty Investor (Non-immigrants)

The United States has signed international trade and investment treaties with many different countries. These treaties allow citizens of another country the opportunity to obtain the E-1 Treaty Trader or E-2 Treaty Investor Visas to temporarily reside and work in the US.

Treaty required

All E-1 and E-2 Visas demand that a treaty regarding trade and investment exist between the US and the country from which the owners of the business originate. For a complete list of such investment treaties, please visit the Department of State's website.

E-2 Treaty Investor Visa

E-2 Visas are known as Treaty Investor Visas. They're considered temporary work visas to the US and have the distinction of allowing an investor to launch, own and manage a business in the United States. They also provide the investor with the opportunity to send senior managers or specialists from his or her country to work in the US-based business. E-2 Visas can be used for new businesses or already existing businesses.

There are other distinctions, as well:

- E-2 Visas require that the business is at least 50% owned by people in the investor's home country.

- In order to qualify for an E-2 Visa, the business investment has to be substantial, with investment funds or assets being irrevocably committed and also of sufficient scope to ensure the successful operation of the company.

- The money or assets must be invested in an active commercial business, rather than in a passive investment (such as owning investment bonds).

- The investment in the business must also have the potential to generate income beyond that needed by the investor and family to provide them with living expenses.

Owners who seek E-2 Visas must be coming to the United States to develop and manage the business. Employees who seek E-2 Visas must be citizens of the home country of the principal owners of the business and be employed as executives, supervisors or specialized skill employees.

The E-2 Treaty Investor Visa allows certain foreign national investors and their employees to obtain immigration status in the United States. The status is valid for two years and can be extended indefinitely. The E-2 Visa holder's spouse and children under the age of 21 are eligible to receive derivative E-2 Visa status.

Notes

_____

_____

_____

_____

_____

_____

_____

_____

_____

_____

_____

_____

CHAPTER 3

Legal Entities

A legal entity is an association, corporation, partnership, proprietorship, trust or individual that has legal standing in the eyes of law. A legal entity has legal capacity to enter into agreements or contracts, assume obligations, incur and pay debts, sue and be sued in its own right and to be held responsible for its actions.

Before you move to the US, you need to consider which type of legal entity best suits you according to your needs; it's quite easy to incorporate in the United States.

In this chapter, we'll talk in detail about the three most common types of entities you can form in the United States. The three types of organizations you can register are:

1. Limited Liability Company (LLC)

2. Corporation

3. Limited Partnership (LP)

LLC

A Limited Liability Company can obtain a tax identification number, an EIN employer identification number, open a bank account and do business legally in the US.

You can create an LLC for different objectives. For example, you can create an LLC specifically for one project with a limited timeline, so this business will exist until the project is finished and liquidated. Or you can create an LLC with a huge scope of business that doesn't have a termination day.

The most useful feature of an LLC is that it gives the owners or members limited liability, which means—under most circumstances—protection from the debts and liabilities of the LLC. Another big benefit is that the LLC doesn't have to be run by the rigid rules required of a corporation. This being said, for purposes of control, it's always recommended for the LLC to adopt some of the rules of the corporation.

The LLC doesn't require you to have special meetings or keep extensive corporate records. Also, it's very flexible when it comes to taxes, allowing you to have a lot of options so you can create a tax strategy that works for you. A single-member LLC can be filed as a sole proprietorship. A multiple-member LLC can file as a partnership or as a corporation—either an S corporation or a C corporation. This type of company also offers pass-through taxation, which means profits flow through to the owners, who get taxed on them as individuals. Finally, the LLC can be either member-managed or manager-managed.

Corporation

A corporation is a company that can obtain a tax identification number, an employer identification number (EIN), open a bank account and do business legally in the US.

Corporations must have a board of directors, officers, shareholders, meetings and minutes.

When you form a corporation, it ensures you and your shareholders won't be personally responsible for company debts or liabilities.

Corporations also have more formal maintenance requirements than LLCs, requiring annual meetings with corporate minutes.

The corporation gives you the opportunity to have two main types of ownership or shares: common and preferred. Common shareholders have voting rights and can receive dividends. Shareholders with preferred shares have priority over common shareholders when it comes to receiving dividends, and a pay-out on claims should the corporation become insolvent.

S Corporation

This is a company that is taxed once, with only the shareholders paying taxes on the profits received. This company is limited to 100 shareholders who must be US citizens or residents.

Owners get common stock with voting rights. Everyone who has stock in the company has the right to vote.

C Corporation

This type of company is taxed twice, with the business paying taxes at the corporate level and the shareholders paying taxes on income received. This form of company has no limit on how many shareholders it has, and it isn't limited to US citizens or residents.

The stock is different from an LLC in that owners hold preferred stock with no voting rights but have priority to dividends before common shareholders.

LP

A limited partnership is a company that can obtain a tax identification number, an employer identification number (EIN), open a bank account and do business legally in the US.

The biggest difference between an LP and the other two forms of company is that from the beginning, you're announcing that in this company, there will be limited partners. This limitation can vary from voting rights to operation and decision rights of managing and non-managing members.

DBA

A DBA (Doing Business As) can be registered to separate the entity from your regular business while still operating under the same LLC or Corporation. For example, let's say you have a company in the construction business, and you get a good offer to distribute safety equipment supplies. However, you don't want to go through the trouble and expense of creating a new LLC or Corporation. What you can do is create a DBA with a name that's more appealing to the new line of business.

What next?

Accountants

When setting up any of the previously mentioned forms of company, it's in your best interest to have an experienced, capable person handling your finances. And don't worry about the expense—the right person will add value (by saving you time and money) from the get-go.

Professional accountants are recognized by two different designations: Certified Public Accountants (CPAs) or Chartered Accountants (CAs). These are highly qualified professionals who have completed degree-level studies, workplace experience and a professional competence program.

Of course, you can hire accountants who aren't certified, chartered or registered, but in my opinion, this is a poor business decision. Tasks such as bookkeeping, tax preparation and general financial management may not require a certified or chartered accountant, but you'll probably be in trouble should your company ever get audited.

Also, remember that your accountant will become intimately involved with the operation of your company. You'll need one you can trust, who has enough experience and who will be there when you need them.

Good accountants help companies grow by managing complex financial work and offering advice on practical business issues. This will most assuredly save you money in the short- and long-term. Choose a CPA or CA carefully and wisely, and you won't go wrong.

Estate planning

Consider estate planning as a way to eliminate many of the uncertainties and tough decisions your loved ones will need to make after you die or become incapacitated. It's also a great way to hang onto and protect the money your investment(s) will earn. Find a good financial advisor or utilize the knowledge of your CPA or CA to guide you through the process. An estate lawyer is also a good person to have on your team.

Wills

The initial and most important step in protecting those you love is to make a will. It's the cornerstone of your estate plan. I've included this section of the chapter because of the terrible consequences of dying without a will, the main one being that the government gets to decide who your beneficiaries are and how your assets will be divided.

A will needs to be clearly indicative of your wishes, easy for your executor to find and easily verified by the courts (probate). You must clearly state who your executor is, who gets your assets, and at what age the beneficiaries will receive their inheritance. There should also be instructions for your burial and funeral. And, if you have dependent children, you really should name a guardian.

Keep your will in an easy-to-find, secure place—like a fire safe or safety deposit box—and tell your executor where it can be found.

POAs

A Power of Attorney (POA) is crucial should you become unable to make your own decisions because of illness or injury. POAs vary from state to state, but they generally authorize a family member or trusted friend to make financial decisions for you when you're unable to do so yourself. Think about what might happen to your business investments if you were temporarily in a coma or had dementia.

As an aside, you may also grant a power of attorney for health care decisions. This is known as a living will, and it helps determine how you would like to be treated if you're incapacitated.

Life insurance

Life insurance can be used in different ways, depending on your financial situation. For example, a young family with a new mortgage might carry life insurance to pay off debts (mortgage, car, credit cards) and replace lost earning potential. For someone older, life insurance can be a powerful estate planning tool—a way to leave a legacy or pay taxes, so your loved ones don't have to.

I'm a firm believer in term life insurance. It's cost-effective and pays out a lump sum should you die during the term of the policy, which is usually 5, 10 or 20 years. Because term life is only renewable at a higher cost at the end of each term, it's best to buy these policies when you're young so that you can lock in the best rates before inevitable health problems show up. You should also need less and less insurance as you build wealth. Therefore, the rising cost of insurance as you age can be offset by the reduced amount of coverage needed.

Planned giving

It's becoming quite common for a parent to give a child some or all of their inheritance in advance of their death.

Giving cash gifts while you're still alive may reduce the overall tax burden on your estate when you die. And when you give cash to adult children, there are no taxes payable, either by you or your child.

This is true for cash only. If you set your child up with investments or real estate, the IRS will deem the asset(s) sold at fair market value, and you'll be expected to pay capital gains taxes where applicable. It's not all bad news, though, as any assets you give to your child and pay capital gains taxes on won't have to pass through probate when you die.

Probate and taxes

Probate is the legal validation of a will, and all estates are subject to some form of it. Some states charge a flat fee for probate, while others base the fee on the size of your estate. Your estate planner's job is to help you structure the estate to minimize fees and taxes on death.

Some things to consider…

- A house owned and lived in by two spouses won't go through probate. On the death of one partner, his or her portion of the asset passes directly to the survivor. A jointly held investment account is treated the same way.

- When an asset isn't held jointly with your spouse, the government generally deems it sold at fair market value when you die. Your estate must then pay capital gains taxes on any appreciation.

- In terms of asset preservation, I feel it's also important to understand that right of survivorship doesn't apply for an adult child whose name is added to a property deed. On your death, he or she becomes a full co-owner of the asset. This means that if that child becomes involved in a lawsuit, bankruptcy or divorce, the asset could be at risk.

- So-called death taxes are usually a much bigger deal than probate fees. The easiest way to reduce or defer such taxes is to name your spouse as the beneficiary on your registered accounts.

Trusts

A trust is a legal entity. It holds assets for a beneficiary whom you name. A trustee distributes those assets according to your instructions. For example, you could have the trustee pay the beneficiary a pre-determined amount monthly, annually, etc., so the inheritance isn't depleted all at once. You can also control the way the assets are used—for education, to purchase a home or even as retirement income.

Creating and administering a trust can be quite expensive, though. So, unless your family has a high net worth or faces unusual ongoing expenses, a will is usually sufficient.

Important Note

You should consider revising updating your plan whenever a significant life event occurs—a birth, a child passes into adulthood, he or she buys a home, you get divorced, there's a death in the family, your investment portfolio changes significantly, your executor moves, etc.

Notes

_____

_____

_____

_____

_____

_____

_____

_____

_____

_____

_____

_____

CHAPTER 4

Alliances

Globalization has changed us into a company that searches the world, not just to sell or to source, but to find intellectual capital— the world's best talents and greatest ideas.

—Jack Welch

1. Chambers of Commerce

Why belong to a chamber of commerce? Because when you help your community, you help yourself.

The most important chamber is the United States Chamber of Commerce (USCC). It has been working for businesses for more than 100 years. The USCC is a business-oriented American lobbying group. Politically, this chamber usually supports Republican political candidates, although it has occasionally supported conservative Democrats. It's also the largest lobbying group in the US.

Chambers of commerce exist at the federal, state, regional and local levels.

All chambers of commerce have the same goals in mind: They represent businesses in the community and give customer referrals to new members of the chamber. They give access to their members for networking and leadership development. They have a specific area for economic development and have community promotions.

One very important thing about chambers of commerce is that all companies are treated the same no matter their size, number of employees or line of business.

Chambers of commerce help you communicate who you are and what you do, which I believe is very important when you're starting a business in a new community.

As an example of how a chamber of commerce can work and market you, consider the following story. A chamber that had 92 restaurants as members made a cookbook that included one recipe from each restaurant. Each company's business name and logo were included so as to promote all the restaurants in the chamber. The books were given to hotels in the area to promote commerce. The impact of the marketing was such that TV stations called chefs to take part in special programs and to teach cooking on local news programs.

2. Family offices

The family office is a best kept secret of successful entrepreneurs to improve their quality of living. There are three types of family offices:

a. **The multi-family office** - operates for a group of families, typically within financial institutions.

b. **The single-family office** - operates exclusively for one family.

c. **The embedded family office** - operates within the conglomerate of the family.

These offices give privacy to families as they administer assets, manage risk and introduce new approaches to investing. Their main purpose is to align interest between clients in the financial system. In most cases, they also give family support—meaning they will pay the bills, take care of their estate planning, security and protection, as well as planning events and trips for the family.

Note: in my opinion, you should only set up a family office if you have over $20 million of assets to invest, otherwise the carrying cost might be too great.

3. Investment summits or forums

Investment summits or forums are alliance-building events from world-class entrepreneurs, investors and experts. Such events are typically held once a year and are often held in different locations. A summit or forum can be as specialized as you need it to be. For example, it can target your industry specifically, or it can be open for worldwide investors. In the select US investment, summit is the most important for investors and is done in Washington.

Most summits or forums have pitch tanks for companies that are looking for investors, which in most cases are entrepreneurs looking for capital to grow their companies.

Franchise summits specialize in putting together all the franchisors, so you can talk to a lot of companies in one place. These types of business alliances are very useful for international investors just starting to invest in the United States because it helps them get the right structure up front.

Many universities in the United States have programs and summits you can attend—even if you're not part of the university. All of these programs are great sources of information, and if you go to economic forums with the most renowned persons in the world, you can really get a feeling of what to expect in the years to come.

4. Strategic Alliances

Strategic alliances are agreements formed between independent companies for the purpose of manufacturing, developing or selling products and services (or other business objectives).

In a strategic alliance, two companies might combine their capabilities, core competencies and resources to improve product or service design, manufacture or distribution.

Types of Strategic Alliances

There are three distinct types of strategic alliances: Equity Strategic Alliance, Joint Venture and Non-Equity Strategic Alliance.

- **Equity Strategic Alliance**

  An equity strategic alliance occurs when one company purchases an equity percentage of the other company. For example, if Company A purchases 40% of the equity in Company B, an equity strategic alliance would be formed.

- **Joint Venture**

  A joint venture occurs when parent companies establish a new and distinct company. Further, if Company A and Company B each own 50% of the child company, it's then referred to as a 50-50 Joint Venture. If Company A owns 30% and Company B owns 70%, then the new company becomes a Majority-owned Venture.

- **Non-Equity Strategic Alliance**

  A non-equity strategic alliance occurs when two or more companies sign a contract to form a relationship that pools their resources and capabilities.

Understanding Strategic Alliances

To understand the reasons for strategic alliances, one needs to consider three different product life cycles. They are the Slow Cycle, Standard Cycle, and Fast Cycle. You see, product life cycle is driven by the particular need to innovate and continually create new products in a given industry. Some industries have a slow life cycle (like the pharmaceutical industry), whereas others (like the book industry or the computer software industry) have a fast life cycle. And the reasons for strategic alliances are different for each type of life cycle:

- **Slow Cycle**

    In a slow cycle, competitive business advantages are protected for long periods of time. Using the example from above, consider that the pharmaceutical industry's products aren't developed yearly, and patents last a long time. They operate in a slow cycle.

    Strategic alliances in this type of industry are made in order to establish a franchise in a new market, access to a restricted market and help maintain market stability.

- **Standard Cycle**

    In a standard cycle, new products are launched every few years, and the company may not be able to maintain its leading position.

    Strategic alliances in this type of industry are made in order to capture market share, establish economies of scale, gain access to complementary resources, push out other companies and pool resources for large capital projects.

43

- **Fast Cycle**

  In a fast cycle, competitive advantages aren't protected, and companies need to constantly develop new products or services to survive (think "publish or perish" or software that is obsolete the moment it hits the marketplace).

  Strategic alliances in this kind of industry are made in order to speed up the development of new goods or services, overcome uncertainty, share research and development expenses and streamline market penetration.

Strategic alliances create value by:

1. Changing the competitive environment (for example, creating new technology standards).

2. Ease of entry and exit (for example, slowly taking over a company and allowing it to exit the industry).

3. Improving current operations (for example, sharing risk and costs).

Challenges

Although strategic alliances create value, there are also significant challenges to consider:

- Partners may fail to commit the resources and capabilities promised.

- Partners may misrepresent what they bring to the table.

- The provided resources may not be used effectively.

- There may be uneven commitments by the various partners.

Notes

_____

_____

_____

_____

_____

_____

_____

_____

_____

_____

_____

_____

_____

CHAPTER 5

Analysis

The ultimate authority must always rest with the individual's own reason and critical analysis.

–Dalai Lama

Analyzing an investment opportunity

Purpose

In order to make a useful analysis of your proposed investment, you must first know the purpose of your investment. For example, if you want to move to the United States to live and become either a resident or a citizen, do you want to make alliances with a US company to expand your business, or do you want to invest to increase your cash flow or capital?

Understanding how your long-term goals align with that of the company you're looking at is crucial. With that in mind, I'm going to show you the easiest way to analyze a company in a few simple steps.

Facts

When investigating a company, always be prepared to ask, "Why?" Also, ask great questions designed to get you the facts you need, like those that follow…

- Who will be your business partners, and what is their reputation?

- How long has the company been in business? What is its niche?

- Is there potential for growth?

- What factors exist that could hurt the business, and why does it have these vulnerabilities?

- Is the company's accounting reliable?

- Is the legal structure something you feel comfortable with?

- Depending on the purpose of your investment, is this type of entity something that works for you, and can it help you to realize your immigration goals?

Symptoms

You must then analyze the business situation, competition, governmental regulations, market and potential for expansion. Ask questions designed to uncover symptoms of existing problems…

- Where is the company headed? Why?

- Do the board members look toward the future in the same way you do? If not, why not?

- Since they're quite literally the company in which you're considering investing, how are the personnel treated? Are they happy? What are their working conditions like? Do they look forward to expanding the business?

- What are the technological capabilities of the business? Is its technology development strategy aligned with yours? How willing is the management team to adapt to new technologies?

- Do you trust the accountants and the way they run things on a daily basis?

- Do the shareholders keep their accounting completely separate from the corporation?

- Are the shares guaranteeing any loans?

- Has any company launched success lawsuits against this one, and what was the reason for those lawsuits?

These are not all the questions you need to ask, by any means, so if anything is still bothering you, remember to ask, "Why?"

S.W.O.T.

In 2011, I was introduced to the S.W.O.T. method of analysis when I attended Harvard executive education for my real estate development program. In 2012-2013, I acquired a Masters AD2 degree at the Instituto Panamericano de Alta Dirección de Empresa (I.P.A.D.E.), where I became an introduction teacher for new students on case analysis for three years in a row. In 2016, we used the same method at the London Business School, where I took my infrastructure finance courses. Today, I share it with you because I believe it's the greatest method for analyzing any kind of new investment. In this case, it will open up your eyes to see where you're going and if you're on the right path.

After gathering all the facts pertaining to the company in which you want to invest, you must make a **S.W.O.T.** analysis. It will provide you with a better understanding of the reality of the business and the **strengths**, **weaknesses**, **opportunities** and **threats** that might exist there. You can even expand your analysis to a state or a country if needed.

What **strengths** does the company offer you, and what do you offer to the company? Ask questions like the following…

- Is this business in the right niche for me?
- What am I bringing to the plate that will move this company forward?

- What do the customers love about the company and its products or services?

- What are the company's most positive brand attributes?

- How well is the brand recognized in the community?

- What is the company's position within the marketplace, and what about that position makes it unique for me as an investor?

- How stable is the supply chain?

- What resources can the company access that its competitors can't?

You must also analyze all the **weaknesses** that could exist, from marketing to product to the actual market. Some questions you might consider are...

- Do I feel comfortable investing in and trusting this company?

- Is the company in the right place at the right time doing the right thing? Is it in the proper market? For example, one question you might ask could be, "Are the products or services affordable for consumers targeted?"

- What kind of employee turnaround is there?

- Are the employees satisfied with their workload and wages?

- What do the customers dislike about the company and its products or services?

- What problems or complaints are often mentioned in negative reviews?

- Which products or services do customers cancel?

- What could the company do better?

- What are the most negative brand attributes?

- What are the biggest obstacles/challenges in the current sales funnel?

- What resources do the competitors have that this company doesn't?

What **opportunities** do you see in this line of business? Ask questions like…

- Is the company utilizing a good tax strategy? In other words, are many investors diversifying their portfolio with the company as part of their tax strategy?

- How are you going to leverage the alliances that board members have built over the years?

- What other opportunities can I see that the administration hasn't seen? Can I take advantage of them to make this company grow?

- How can the company improve its sales and customer support processes?

- What kind of messaging resonates with the customers?

- How can the company further engage its most vocal brand advocates?

- Is the company allocating departmental resources effectively?

- Are there budgets, tools or other resources the company isn't leveraging fully?

- Which advertising channels exceeded the company's expectations, and why?

You must also analyze all the **threats** to your business. Ask questions such as...

- Does the business have a license that expires?

- Do I need special permits?

- Is the market at the end of the cycle or at the beginning?

- Can I expand the business to different states?

- What applicable laws are different in those states?

- Do I need a different lawyer for each state?

- Is the CEO at a certain age or suffering from a health condition that makes me feel uncomfortable?

- Has the competition saturated the market?

- Are there important barriers to entry in the market?

Problems

When you're finished with the S.W.O.T. analysis, you should investigate any problems you've discovered the company has. For example:

- Are there any problems with administration? If so, how long have these problems been there, and how can they be fixed?

- Are there problems in other departments? How did the company get where it is with these problems? Are they fixable? Can you prevent such things from happening in the future?

- If you plan to live in the United States, does this company help you with your immigration status? Can this change?

Solutions

And after going through the process of analysis, you need to evaluate each possible alternative or solution available to you, depending on your ability and resources.

You must also be prepared to take action and make things happen. If you don't, you'll have wasted valuable time and resources.

The six steps illustrated in the diagram below demonstrate the entire analytical process we've been discussing.

1. Define your **Purpose**

2. Ask questions to ascertain the **Facts**

3. Identify any **Symptoms** your work has uncovered

4. Perform a **S.W.O.T.** analysis

5. List the **Problems** as you see them

6. Come up with **Solutions** for those problems

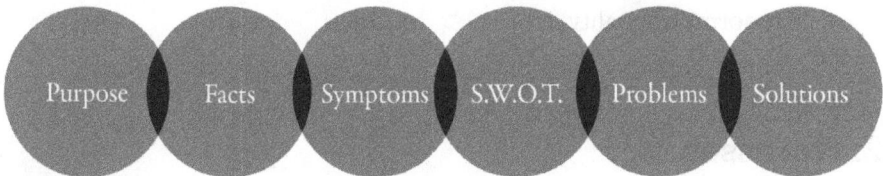

Other strategic analysis tools

Critical Success Factor (CSF) analysis is a technique used to identify areas in which a business must succeed in order to achieve its mission.

To achieve its goals, the assembled team needs to come up with approximately 10-15 key success factors that are then personalized depending on the affected department. Each factor is worked to achieve success for the company based on standards and rules that need to be followed using identified algorithms to guarantee better service for clients and partners.

It's well-known that there are a number of basic key success factors that fall under five dominant strategies. The specific goal of working each factor would, of course, be identifiable qualitative (efficient) or quantitative (profitable) results.

1. Plan

- Access to financial resources
- Balanced budget
- Project chart, goals, roles and impacts
- Realistic calendar of tasks and activities
- Set norms of quality

2. Processes

- Formal work methodology
- Solid infrastructures

3. People

- Commitment
- Competencies
- Teamwork

4. Power

- Experienced managers
- Sense of fairness

Contingency strategy

- Risk and vulnerability assessment

  Scenario Planning is a technique used for identifying a number of plausible scenarios or assumptions regarding what might happen in the future of a business.

  Porter's Five Forces provides a framework for analyzing strength and weakness in five fundamental factors that affect competition in every industry: potential entrants, competitors, buyers, suppliers and alternative products or services. This structure allows for the determination of corporate strategy regarding the previously mentioned influences.

  PESTLE analysis is a technique used for understanding variable external influences that may affect a business.

An example of PESTLE analysis

PESTLE analysis is a fundamental tool you can use for business strategy and planning. It helps you assess the environment of a business and its possible impact on the performance of that company.

PESTLE is an acronym for **six external factors** that can affect a business: Political, Economic, Sociological, Technological, Legal and Environmental. Each factor can profoundly affect a business, with varying implications. Some of those implications are:

- **Duration of Impact** – short-term or long-term

- **Rate of Impact** – unknown, increasing, decreasing or unchanged

- **Importance** – unknown, unimportant, important or critical

- **Type of Change** – unknown, positive or negative

The following **PESTLE analysis example** clarifies how external factors work and what type of information you should include in your analysis; it involves investing in a company in the US from outside that country.

Category	Political	Economic	Sociological	Technological	Legal	Environmental
Possible factors	Migratory treaties.	Printing too much money. Possible recession or even depression.	Consumer preferences. Millennial vs baby boomer marketing.	New technologies. Online marketing. Automation	Licensing regulations. Treaties.	COVID-19
Business Impact	TMEC barriers or accesses.	Governmental overspending. Increasing interest rates.	Product tropicalization.	Copyrights. Brand registration. Patents.	Tropicalize and cope with regulation.	Business closures. Business redevelopment.
Duration of Impact	Unknown	12-24 months. Long-term.	6-12 months. Short-term.	0-6 months. Short-term.	Constant. Long-term.	Short-term.
Type of Change	Stable. Positive.	Unstable. Negative.	Predictable. Positive.	Negative.	Negative.	Negative.
Rate of impact	Stable. Unchanged.	Long-term.	Predictable with studies	Unknown.	Variable. Increasing / Decreasing	Variable. Increasing / Decreasing
Importance	Important.	Important.	Very important.	Important.	Critical.	Critical.

Advantages of PESTLE analysis

PESTLE is a great tool for helping you understand how external factors affect the business you're analyzing. It can:

- determine the long-term effect of external factors on the performance and activities of the business.

- evaluate the risks associated with the markets in which you're interested.

- gain a strategic advantage over competitors.

- identify solutions to problems.

- review any strategies that are already in place.

- work out a new vision or direction, invent a new product or outline an innovative plan for the business in question.

PESTLE is an extended version of PEST analysis. It's most often used in conjunction with other analytical business tools like **S.W.O.T. analysis** and Porter's Five Forces to give a clear understanding of a given situation and related internal and external factors.

Analysis of a business isn't easy, but it's imperative that you do your homework. Careful observation and recording of results can be the difference between a good investment and a bad one.

Case Study: Analysis of the Allied Orion Group

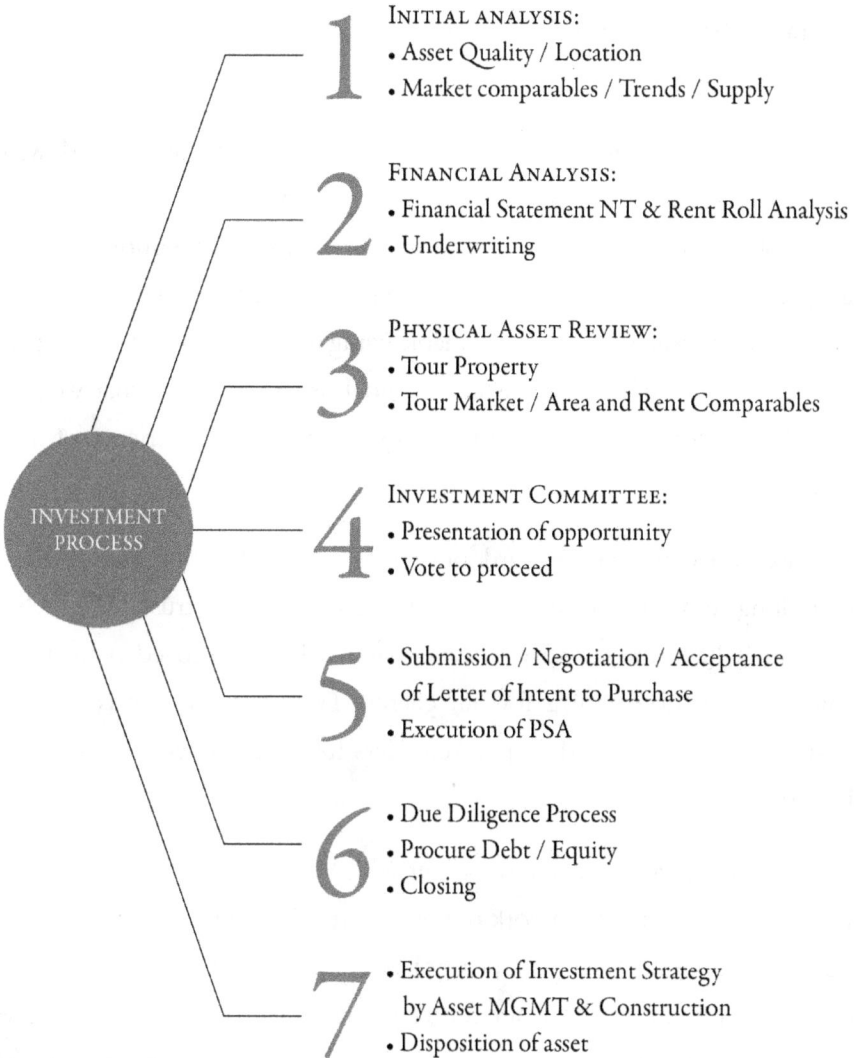

ALLIED ORION GROUP

1
INITIAL ANALYSIS:
- Asset Quality / Location
- Market comparables / Trends / Supply

2
FINANCIAL ANALYSIS:
- Financial Statement NT & Rent Roll Analysis
- Underwriting

3
PHYSICAL ASSET REVIEW:
- Tour Property
- Tour Market / Area and Rent Comparables

4
INVESTMENT COMMITTEE:
- Presentation of opportunity
- Vote to proceed

INVESTMENT PROCESS

5
- Submission / Negotiation / Acceptance of Letter of Intent to Purchase
- Execution of PSA

6
- Due Diligence Process
- Procure Debt / Equity
- Closing

7
- Execution of Investment Strategy by Asset MGMT & Construction
- Disposition of asset

One of the companies I've invested in is the Allied Orion Group. The following section describes our investment outlook and is a great example of a document that can assist in your analysis of a company.

We believe that thoroughly understanding the needs of our residents is the key to our success. To succeed in the dynamic industry of providing homes, it's imperative that we challenge ourselves and remain diligent with our pursuit of resident satisfaction.

Our culture and business ethics are guided by our values: hard work, integrity, excellence and teamwork. We're determined to fully utilize the talents of our team members, and to encourage the contributions that they can provide. We believe that by unifying and collaborating we can create synergies that result in a more sustainable living experience. We, as a company, have committed fully to the sustainable goal of remembering that we strive to do "whatever it takes" to create the most out of the experience of living with us.

As we move forward toward our goals, we're directing our focus on these long-term ideals: innovation, performance and trust. We believe these goals have the capacity to renew and deliver improved performance while we maximize returns for our clients. Trust becomes the cornerstone of future partnerships with our stakeholders that will propel us forward into the future.

To that note, we're excited to partner with Stateside Capital Partners, who will look to expand our network of business relationships overseas, including those in the GCC (Gulf Cooperation Council) member states. We look forward to providing all of our future partners with the same unparalleled service and diligence that have made Allied Orion Group what we are today.

Our story

Allied Orion Group is a leading fully integrated, multi-family real estate investment, construction and property management firm headquartered in Houston, Texas with additional offices in Denver, Dallas and San Antonio.

History of risk-adjusted returns

Allied Orion Group has a long history of successful multi-family development, investment and asset management, including property management through all real estate cycles. In its private investment activities, the company has realized a weighted-average project-level return of 21.77% over the last twenty years, with institutional partners such as Carlyle, GE Capital, AmStar, State Farm, Related and HQ Capital.

Disciplined investment process utilizing fully-integrated synergies

- The Investment team at Allied Orion Group has over 60 years of combined experience in the development, acquisition and disposition of multi-family properties.

- Allied Orion's Property Management Division currently has in excess of 24,000 units under its supervision, spanning seven states, which provides us with a competitive market advantage, as we already have an educated understanding of those markets and their constantly evolving dynamics.

- Allied Orion Group's Construction Division has been involved in the construction and/or rehabilitation of nearly 18,000 units with a total aggregate value of approximately $1.5 billion. This, again, provides Allied Orion with a competitive advantage in evaluating the risks and costs involved with either renovating or maintaining potential acquisitions.

- Additionally, Allied Orion Group's Advisory Board is comprised of 3 members with over 100 years of combined acquisition and development experience.

- Overall, the company has unparalleled credentials and experience managing all the components of the investment process, from origination, underwriting/due diligence, financing, capital improvements, asset repositioning, refinancing and/or disposition.

I. INVESTMENT TYPES

- Development Deals

- Joint Ventures

- Mezzanine Debt

- Note Purchases

- Outright Acquisitions

- Preferred Equity

II. INVESTMENT CRITERIA

- Number of Units: 150 units and larger

- Year of Construction: 2001 and newer

- Leverage: 65-75% LTV

- Investment Horizon: 3 to 7 years

- Asset Class: Class A+ to Class B

Core core-plus value-add

- Stabilized Cash-On-Cash

- (Over Hold Period)

- 7-9% 8-10%+ 9-11%+

- Return on Capital Investments N/A 20%+ 25%+

- IRR to LP 12%+ 14%+ 16%+

III. ADDITIONAL INVESTMENT REQUIREMENTS

- Properties without functional obsolescence including, but not limited to, single-paned, non-Energy Star compliant windows, boiler/chiller systems, sub-9' ceilings, non-ADA compliant, etc.

- Amenities are in-line with, or can be cost-efficiently brought up to, market comparable standards. These include: swimming pools with cabanas, grilling/common areas, package delivery/locker systems, dog park/spa, car charging stations, bike rooms, dry clean pick-up/ delivery, golf simulators, alternate work spaces, specialized class offerings (yoga, Pilates, etc.), and UBER/ Lyft waiting stations.

ACQUISITIONS

IV. STRATEGIC MULTI-FAMILY INVESTMENT RATIONALE

Allied Orion Group's acquisition investment strategy focuses on acquiring tangible and operational assets with intrinsic collateral and land value at prices below replacement cost. Our fully-integrated structure allows us to utilize the knowledge and experience of our Executive Committee, Investment, Property Management and Construction divisions to provide highly-synergized analyzes of potential acquisition opportunities and the risks involved with each.

- **Resiliency/downside protection.** Multi-family properties have historically exhibited greater resiliency in maintaining asset values and experienced lower volatility with market rents and occupancy levels relative to other property types (retail, office, industrial, etc.).

- **Home ownership trends.** Due to changes in lifestyle and more stringent underwriting standards, home ownership rates have fallen, thus increasing the demand for rental units.

- **Demographic shifts.** The Millennial Generation consists of 85 million US citizens, born between 1981 through 1993, which is larger than the Baby Boomer Generation. With 57% of the population under the age of 34 renting, the demand for Multi-family and rental properties is expected to continue.

- **Favorable risk-reward balance.** Some cycles and locations may favor either buying existing assets or building new construction to obtain the most favorable risk adjusted returns.

- **Socially responsible investments.** Typically complies with most investors socially responsible investment requirements including Sharia principles.

V. VALUE DRIVERS

The following are seven factors that we look for in identifying potential acquisitions, all of which lead to sustained rent growth and occupancy level opportunities:

1. **Job growth.** Current and projected job creation above the national average.

2. **Population growth.** Current and expected future population growth above the national average.

3. **Positive location trends.** Properties located in areas or sub-markets experiencing and projected to experience urban transformation, including new infrastructure, transportation, employment centers, retail or educational facilities.

4. **Supply-constrained markets.** Markets and submarkets with constrained supply and high barriers to entry, including restrictive zoning or entitlements (land use, product types or density), unavailability of developable land or utilities capacity, etc.

5. **Favorable renting economics.** High price-to-rent ratio, comparing median home prices and mortgage payments to median rents.

6. **High absorption markets.** Markets with reduced time for new housing brought to the market to be purchased or rented.

7. **Positive historical performance.** We thoroughly evaluate property and sub-market performance, especially during times of significant adverse conditions, including vacancy rate and lease trends.

VI. PRODUCT TYPES

- **Affordable:** Properties with a percentage of units with certain affordability standards (i.e. median household income at or below certain level rated by the national government).

- **Conventional:**

  - **Garden/walk-up:** Typically, three or four stories, walk-up multi-family housing draws its name from its lack of an elevator. It also relies on on-grade parking solutions, either in surface lots or tucked under the wooden structure.

  - **Wrap:** Wrap buildings consist of residential units and/or retail "wrapping" around an above-grade parking structure. Generally appropriate for sites where more expensive below-grade parking is not an option; the wrap building offers a good high-density solution on sites two acres or larger.

- **Podium:** Podium buildings are generally wood construction sitting atop concrete parking or mixed use, which provides a cost-effective alternative to more expensive concrete and steel buildings.

It's important to note, while Wrap and/or Podium properties may contain a ground-floor retail (mixed-use) element, those are not opportunities we are currently targeting in the post-COVID-19 landscape.

VII. INVESTMENT STRATEGIES/ASSET TYPES

- **Core:** Stabilized assets which require little or no renovation and very little asset management. Core property tenants tend to be more white-collar, and are usually renters by choice. These properties tend to be in major urban centers with high demand. Typically, they're one to five years old and offer high-end finishes and fixtures with a full spectrum of the newest and most desirable amenities in the industry. These assets are typically classified as "A+."

- **Core-plus:** Similar to Core Assets, but often needing light improvements to the units or amenities, management efficiencies or by increasing the quality of the tenants. Similar to Core properties, these properties tend to be of high quality and historically well-occupied. The potential downside of a Core Plus investment is that the cash flow is less predictable than a core investment, and require active participation by ownership. A 15-year-old apartment building that is well occupied but in need of light upgrades is an example of a Core Plus investment opportunity. The property will produce ample cash flow but some of the cash will be used for future deferred maintenance such as roofs and parking lot repairs. These assets are typically classified as "A" to "A-."

- **Value-add:** Existing assets below replacement cost with observable operational inefficiencies or that have the potential to be brought up to comparable standards through renovation, increasing NOI and ultimately, increasing returns to investors. This strategy involves the identification of well-located assets with depressed operating results caused by poor management and/or capital starvation. These investments should deliver higher overall returns due to the execution risk of the business plan, with less near-term cash distributions due to the need to invest capital in to the property during the early stages of the investment. For our purposes, we would classify these assets as "B" to "B+" in "A" locations.

- **Opportunistic & development:** These properties often have little to no cash flow at acquisition, but have the potential to produce a tremendous amount of cash flow once the value has been added. Opportunistic investors take on the most complicated projects and may not see a return on their investment for three or more years. These investment strategies require years of experience and a team of people to be successful. An example of such an investment would be a ground-up development deal, which is the primary investment strategy that we at Allied Orion have been executing for over 35 years. We've successfully developed nearly 15,000 units across the United States with a total aggregate value of approximately $1.3 billion.

- **Note purchases:** Financial institutions sell non-performing loans to rapidly dispose of unwanted assets, often at a gain to book values. Loan sales reduce expenses related to loan workouts and in some cases, particularly for smaller institutions without dedicated workout teams, are the preferred resolution for troubled assets. We're currently registered with Debt X, the world's largest loan sale platform and continue to monitor for opportunities.

VIII. TARGET MARKETS

The following are the primary location targets for investment opportunities:

Sunbelt states

- The Sunbelt is the fastest growing area of the country and includes Alabama, Arizona, Arkansas, Colorado, Florida, Georgia, Louisiana, New Mexico, Tennessee and Texas.

- Sunbelt markets, specifically those with exhibited consistent growth in population, employment and performance, is where we are seeing the growth opportunities and the new multi-family supply.

- Companies are moving their corporate headquarters to the Sunbelt in search of less inclement weather, affordability and favorable tax treatments in places like Texas, with no state income tax.

Technology/education-driven markets

Austin, Charlotte, Dallas and Denver are a few cities in which we currently manage properties that have consistently ranked at, or near, the top of various "Best of" lists for job growth, real estate investment, labor markets, etc., which have both a major research-focused university and a vibrant technology start-up environment. We're looking for opportunities in other markets with similar dynamics where we have no current management presence, such as Ann Arbor (Michigan), Atlanta (Georgia), Huntsville (Alabama), Phoenix (Arizona), Pittsburgh (Pennsylvania) and Raleigh/Durham (North Carolina), which have been some of the top-performing markets in the US in population/ job growth, primarily driven by technology and research, over the last few years.

Again, while Ann Arbor and Pittsburgh are Midwestern states, they exhibit many of the same characteristics we see in the identified Sunbelt target markets, including a lower cost of living, exhibited job growth and a migration of tech employers moving to the region to capitalize on the locally-grown tech talent pool.

Existing management presence

We're looking at opportunities in states where we have an established property management presence, which gives us deep insights and perspective of the market/submarket and helps us to identify comparable supply, drivers and trends. Our current Property Management portfolio consists of approximately 24,000+ units in seven states across the Sunbelt region of the United States: Of those states, Alabama, Colorado, North Carolina and Texas all have cities which have multiple characteristics indicative of attractive markets outlined in this document.

- Alabama
- Arkansas
- Louisiana

- North Carolina

- Colorado

- Florida

- Texas

Opportunities presented by market disruptions and financial stress due to COVID

Allied Orion Group anticipates the current COVID-19 pandemic will present opportunities in which we could capture outsized risk-adjusted returns during the economic fallout and the recovery period. In response to this unfolding situation, the company is monitoring appropriate investment positions at all levels of the capital structure that will be available as markets begin to stabilize.

The current economic environment, specifically as it relates to the oil industry, has led to a reduced focus on acquisition opportunities in Houston for the short to mid-term. The same can be said for the cities of Orlando and Las Vegas, where COVID-19 has essentially brought the hospitality industry to a halt. It will be some time until those cities begin to recover from this crisis. That being said, we will continue to search for and evaluate any potential opportunities in those and other similarly affected markets, including some of which may not be in the Sunbelt region, but meet a number of our criteria.

Note: summaries describing the aforementioned cities, how those cities rank in a number of "Best of" lists, percentage of rent vs own and how they compare to the national medians for average home prices and rental amounts are available from the company but are beyond the scope of this book.

IX. MULTI-FAMILY PERFORMANCE DURING ADVERSE ECONOMIC ENVIRONMENTS

Investor perspective

Strong fundamentals and inelastic demand support the multi-family apartment sector in the post-COVID-19 pandemic era:

- Multi-family has historically shown resiliency during down-market cycles.

- US multi-family property rents declined less than half of office and industrial properties during the 2001 economic recession and their growth rate was considerably higher post-recession.

- During the 2008-2009 recession, multi-family rents were more resilient than those of office, industrial and retail.

- Multi-family rents have outperformed those of the other major property sectors during and after the 2008-2009 recession in three ways: The sector experienced the lowest level of rent decline, the fastest recovery to pre-recession peaks and the longest post-recession period of rent growth.

Multi-family industrial office and retail

People are likely to save cash and cut spending. The retail, office and hospitality sectors are negatively impacted as people stop visiting stores for discretionary goods and services, companies shutter and people travel less often. But people will continue to need a place to live.

During a time where liquidity is important, most people will not look to buy homes, which is a major purchase. In fact, it can be more challenging for people to qualify for mortgages during a recession as lenders typically originate less loans due to liquidity constraints and more carefully scrutinize mortgage loan applications. Therefore, it's likely that the share of renters will increase during these uncertain times.

The collapse of the financial system during the Great Recession, which began in December 2007 and lasted until June 2009, froze credit and spending, impacting consumer and investor confidence. During this time, apartment Real Estate Investment Trusts (REITs) experienced volatility as much as other investments, but quickly rebounded. Over the subsequent five years after the Great Recession, apartment REITs outpaced other commercial real estate classes and the S&P 500.

Looking back over the course of four decades, residential rents throughout the US have generally risen each year—even during recessions, according to the US Bureau of Labor Statistics. The one exception is the period following the Great Recession from 2009 to 2010, when the pace of rent growth was flat.

Following that year, however, rents quickly continued their ascent. Rents make up the bulk of the gross revenue for apartment buildings, so as rents rise, so does gross revenue. For building owners with fixed rate mortgages and stable expenses, that would mean it's possible for net operating incomes to rise as well, which ultimately equals rising property values.

Another measure of the performance of multi-family investments is the vacancy levels in the industry.

Rental vacancy in the US has generally increased during past recessions, but not dramatically. It's widely noted that the Great Recession was the most financially devastating period since the Great Depression in the 1930s, and even then, the vacancy rate for US rentals only peaked at approximately 10.6% in 2009 before falling steeply in the following years, according to the US Census Bureau information.

Additionally, certain markets suffered far less dramatic falls in vacancy rates during the Great Recession, which demonstrates that there can be good opportunities in all market environments as long as the market fundamentals remain strong.

The Millennial (those born between 1981 and 1996) Effect is also driving the growth of the multi-family market. Increased cost of housing and loans due to student loan burdens, combined with their changing lifestyle expectations—for example, their desire for mobility, preference for collecting experiences versus material possessions and desire for the amenities and services offered by cities—have resulted in more millennials continuing to rent, and choosing to do so in core urban areas and near-in suburbs, where they're willing to trade square footage for a convenient location.

This trend appears likely to continue with the post-millennial generation, the oldest of whom are now graduating from college and entering the workforce, as they demonstrate the same preference for an urban lifestyle.

National homeownership rates continue to trail historical numbers, with the under age-35 rate falling from a peak of 43% in 2007 to 37% at the end of 2018. Tighter borrowing regulations, the growing affordability spread between rental and home ownership, delayed child-bearing and household setup, flexibility and mobility afforded by renting and the attractiveness of the lifestyle aspects of cities are driving millennials away from home ownership to remain long-term renters.

Current landscape

The COVID-19 pandemic is changing the way that multi-family properties market their communities, lease and collect rent. Virtual property tours and the ability for tenants to make their payments online via credit cards are examples of how the industry is transitioning. Despite the changes, property managers' mitigation efforts (absorbing transaction fees, waiving credit card payment/late fees, etc.) have kept rent payment rates close to normal, and although leasing activity slowed significantly in April and May, preliminary June numbers indicate a rebound may already be underway.

Notes

_____

_____

_____

_____

_____

_____

_____

_____

_____

_____

_____

_____

CHAPTER 6

What to Expect

Take time to deliberate; but when the time for action arrives, stop thinking and go in.

–Andrew Jackson

Once you've made the decision and have an amazing team put together, you can expect things to flow easily and grow your returns. The US taxation and banking system can help you to increase and keep your capital—if you do your homework. There are many options to do this. I'll just provide a couple of examples I think are important.

Taxation rates

INCOMES AND FEDERAL, STATE & LOCAL TAXES IN 2020

Income Groups			Taxes as % of Income		
Group	Income Range	Average Cash Income	Federal	State & Local	Total
Lowest 20%	< $24,000	$14,000	7.6%	12.8%	20.4%
Second 20%	$24,000 - $43,000	$33,800	11.0%	11.4%	22.4%
Middle 20%	$43,000 - $70,000	$55,000	14.4%	11.1%	25.5%
Fourth	$263,000 - $644,000	$382,600	21.7%	9.3%	31.0%
Top 1%	$644,000 or more	$2,012,400	24.5%	9.9%	34.4%
All		$95,000	19.3%	10.9%	29.5%
Bottom 99%	<$644,000	$80,100	17.9%	10.3%	28.2%

Source: Institute on Taxation & Economic Policy (ITEP), Tax Model July 2020.

Contrary to popular belief, the rich in the United States pay the greatest amount of taxes (see the chart below). Therefore, it behooves you to understand the tax laws well or have a professional on your team who knows the tax laws well. And remember, corporate taxes are eventually borne by the people—that includes you.

Deferring taxes

The US has a 1031 tax-deferred exchange that lets you roll over the taxes until either you die or you decide not to roll them over anymore—a great product for cash flow. But this has to be done through a qualified intermediary. Don't be cheap here. You need to hire someone with a great reputation and who'll get the job done right.

The way the exchange works is you can sell a property and not pay capital gains tax if you exchange it for a similar kind of property within a certain period of time—meaning you have 45 days today to identify a property and 180 days to close. You can either upgrade the property you had or diversify your portfolio into smaller properties. One important thing to remember is you can't touch any of the cash that comes from the sale. If you do, you lose the tax benefit, and you have to pay the taxes.

Gifting of money

The United States also lets you give amounts of cash to different people within a one-year period and without any tax consequence for the beneficiary or you. If you surpass a certain amount, though, you'll need to pay taxes or give it to someone as part of a living inheritance. Your tax accountant and tax attorney will be of great help here.

Estate taxes

The United States is a country where there's an estate tax. The amount varies depending on whether the Democrats or Republicans are in power and the laws passed within that period of time. There are ways that you can plan ahead, though. You can make a trust for your kids, so they can own assets.

You can manage the assets and have administrative control without being the full owner of the asset in the trust. You can also decide at what age or under what circumstances your children can take control of the administration of the assets. Of course, success in these endeavors implies that you have legal advice and a good strategy.

Banking

Most Americans don't understand the US banking system, so imagine how difficult it can be for someone from another country to comprehend such institutions. Here are some basics to get you started...

There are a number of different types of bank in the US:

Commercial Banks provide any number of services like accepting deposits, issuing business loans and offering basic investment products. Their function is to serve the business community rather than the regular population. They rely on lines of credit to manage cash flow.

Credit Unions are member-owned financial cooperatives, controlled by those members to provide credit at competitive interest rates. So, they're non-profit organizations owned by customers for the purpose of offering banking services to them. Credit unions differ in that the members often live in the same area, have similar occupations and places of work.

Mutual Banks are like credit unions in that they're owned by the members or customers instead of non-member investors.

Online Banks operate entirely online and don't have traditional brick and mortar locations you can go to. These are a popular choice in this ever more digitalized world.

Retail Banks are the ones most people use. These banks are consumer-focused, offer a place to deposit money, acquire credit cards and secure loans.

Savings and Loans Associations specialize in accepting savings and deposits, making mortgage and other loans.

Savings Banks provide the basic service of offering a place for people to save and accrue interest on their money.

The Central Bank (Federal Reserve) manages the monetary system of the government. It's responsible for managing economic activity and supervising banks.

How do banks in the US work?

Banks in the US are businesses that make money with the money you put into your bank account. They add your money to a large pool of money that's used for other people to buy homes, cars, finance their business or pay for a child's education. They must return your money on demand, though.

Banks create money in the economy by administering loans. The Federal Reserve regulates the lending of money by setting reserve requirements that indicate the amount of money banks are allowed to lend. They're allowed to lend out 90% of your deposit and can't touch 10% of it. So, if you put $1,000 into your account, $900 goes back out into the economy and eventually gets deposited into another bank. That bank can lend out 90% of the $900 that was put into the account, and so on and so on, creating an exponentially increasing amount of money in the economy.

The Federal Reserve can change rules and regulations as needed to support the economy. For example, if it lowers the required amount of money the banks must hold onto, more cash will be pumped out into the economy (referred to as an expansionary monetary policy). If the federal reserve wants an overheated economy to slow down, it will raise the amount the banks must keep so that less money gets put into the economy (contractionary policy). **Note:** the more money banks can lend out, the greater the earnings they make from your money,

The United States has a great banking system, partly—I believe—because they're very careful with their diligence. And, once you're approved for a loan, it's absolutely worth using their money to grow your business. I'll give a quick example since many of you will already know how it works.

Let's suppose you're planning to make a $1,000,000 investment by yourself. You buy an asset that gives you an 8% return, so you're making $80,000 in income a year. In a second scenario, instead of investing the million dollars, you only invest $500,000 and ask for a loan from a bank for the other half-million dollars. Of course, the bank will charge interest. In this case, it's 3%, so you'll be paying $15,000 a year in interest. Once you deduct that interest from the 8% return, you're left with $65,000 of earnings on your $500,000 investment, which increases your return to 13%. Now, let's go a little further and suppose the bank is willing to lend you $750,000 at the same 3% interest rate. If you still get an 8% return, you've increased your return to 23%. In most cases, this kind of return would be comparable to what most people make in their home countries. Here you can diversify your portfolio, and the same million dollars can be put to work in four different assets making a 23% return.

As of 2020, the 3% or less interest the bank charged you is—for all intents and purposes—free money, so once you reduce inflation and get the tax benefits, you've pretty much got a free ride.

So, what can you expect from investing in the United States? I would say great economic stability, high quality of life for all classes and security for you and your loved ones—but only if you follow the rules and laws. The US has a strong law & order presence, and the country aggressively uses its laws against anyone who doesn't do things the way they're supposed to. The good aspect of such a presence is there are many laws that let you do things the right way to increase capital as well as your returns.

Notes

CHAPTER 7

Make it Happen

"Successful people do what unsuccessful people are not willing to do. Don't wish it were easier; wish you were better."

–Jim Rohn

Getting started

All great successes begin somewhere. It starts with a decision to take action. You can plan all you want, but until you choose a task and do it, all you have is a dream.

Due diligence

One dictionary I looked at defined due diligence as "an investigation, audit or review performed to confirm the facts of a matter under consideration. In the financial world, due diligence requires an examination of financial records before entering into a proposed transaction with another party." Thus part of your analysis before investing in a company needs to be looking hard at its financials.

Another dictionary definition says that due diligence means "the care that a reasonable person exercises to avoid harm to other persons or their property." In terms of our discussion, this means doing your homework and making yourself an expert before purchasing another company.

How do you perform due diligence?

Let's say that you're planning to buy into a particular business. The company interests you because it's perfectly positioned in a high traffic area in a great part of a booming city. However, before you invest anything, you or a professional representative must perform due diligence. The due diligence process includes getting answers to questions similar to the ones listed below:

- Is the cash flow of the company solid? Do the books identify the source of revenue?

- Are financial projections reasonable and accurate?

- What's the size of the market, and what's the company's share within it?

- Is the market thriving, weakening or stagnant? Similarly, are company profits on the increase, or are they declining?

- Are there new competitors in the company's market, or poised to enter the market, that could impact earnings?

- Is the company online, and how does its presence compare to its competitors?

- Are all physical assets valued properly and fairly?

- Are there any liabilities, hidden or otherwise?

- Did you find all pertinent company documents (articles of incorporation, board meeting minutes, tax registration, etc.)?

- Are taxes up to date?

- Does the company lease property? If so, when does the lease end?

- What kinds of insurance coverage are in place?

- Are employee files complete and accurate, including salary and benefits?

Due diligence when purchasing commercial property

- **Building inspection**: Have a qualified building inspector perform the inspection, but you should also search for any liens on the property. If the property is new, have all the contractors been paid?

- **Code compliance**: Is the business in compliance with all building, safety and zoning codes?

- **Environment**: Have hazardous materials like asbestos, lead paint or radon been found on the site? What, if anything, is being done regarding these hazards? Is the property located in a flood zone, on an active fault-line or within a protected environment?

- **Location**: What are the mineral, gas and oil rights to the property, and have they been sold? On average, how much traffic passes by your business in a day? Is it easy to enter and exit the parking lot? Is there sufficient parking?

- **Performance**: This is the time to access profit/loss statements and ask questions regarding the success of the business at the current location.

The cold, hard truth

Due diligence is boring, inconvenient, sometimes expensive and time-consuming. If it doesn't remind you of a visit to the dentist, you probably didn't do it right. A good standard is that you can answer "Yes" to the question, "Do I know as much about this business as I do about my own?"

Note: I've given you a brief overview of due diligence questions you can use as a guide when assessing a business that you're considering. The questions are by no means exhaustive, so first consider the information you need, then determine the right questions to ask and which experts to search out. For example, even if you're in a financial field, you aren't necessarily skilled at evaluating a company's books, so it's better to spend a little money now to hire the right expert now and avoid costly mistakes later.

Creating partnerships

- A partnership offers many benefits like collaboration, equality, reliability, support, teamwork and trust. These benefits and the people who provide them can often make the difference between success and failure. It's not only who you invite into your life, but also how you interact with them.

- A partnership is considered to be two or more people or organizations that work together to solve a common problem while sharing benefits, resources, responsibilities, rewards, risks and skills. It's a form of agreement that must grow to fill the stated needs of the individuals involved.

- Synergistic in nature, partnerships should allow the individuals or organizations involved to leverage their assets—capabilities, client base, expertise and resources.

- Success can't be achieved unless the partnership allows everyone to make continuous improvements. And by collaborating with others, you gain the ability to direct your resources and capabilities as you prioritize projects.

- The Pareto Principle or 80–20 rule specifies that 80% of consequences come from 20% of the causes. That means to achieve more with less, one needs to be selective rather than exhaustive.

- Good leaders strive for excellence in a few key areas they can master, rather than seek top performance across many. Similarly, when you work on creating a competitive advantage, you should focus your resources on what you do best and use others' resources for everything else.

- Companies are ecosystems. They include customers, distributors, employees, investors and service providers who partner with each other to foster long-term relationships.

- Reciprocal partnerships breed long-term success when a few fundamentals are adhered to:

  1. **Develop processes that ensure repeatability:** If something works in a partnership, stick with it. If it doesn't, take another approach. The world moves too fast to make things up as you go.

  2. **Create trackable and measurable reward systems:** Risk-sharing and incentive-based performance are major drivers that keep people and programs moving forward.

  3. **Evolve and expand the ecosystem:** If you take something out, whether it's people, processes or products, something must be put back in. Because a company's motion never stops. Remember, business opportunities often require new innovations, partners and products.

Coming together is a beginning. Keeping together is progress. Working together is success. –Henry Ford

---

A partnership is about the long-term pursuit of mutual needs. All parties must be committed to the same goals and prepared to achieve them by sticking to sound and established principles. However, each partner must also be agile enough to recognize changes that require adaptation of their behavior to stay on track in the long term. It would be helpful if each understands what they contribute to the partnership.

Make your investment grow

1. Be a client-centered business

Identifying client needs and satisfying them helps ensure company growth:

- Know your customers better. Where are they? Who are they? What are their values?

- Conduct direct research based on interviews, focus groups and surveys. Also use secondary sources, like reports or surveys.

- Remember that 80% of your sales will come from 20% of your customers. So, make sure you understand your best customers and cultivate their loyalty.

- Purchase a customer relationship management (CRM) system. It will provide your team with essential information on existing and potential customers.

2. Cultivate talent

Provide better training for current employees, and focus on hiring qualified labor. To put this strategy into action, in my opinion, one needs to do the following:

- Develop a human resources management plan that predicts staffing needs and describes how you're going to retain and motivate employees.

- Assess employee skills to see where there are gaps, then develop training and recruitment strategies to fill them.

- Provide clear job descriptions, performance objectives, appraisals and rewards to ensure your employees are productive and focused on giving their best every day.

3. Innovate

To increase your company's ability to innovate:

- Ask for ideas and feedback from clients, stakeholders and suppliers. You should harness employee creativity, as they're often your best source of ideas.

- Develop an innovation strategy with your team. It should cover improvements to your business model, marketing strategy, processes, products, services and supply chain. Update it at least monthly.

- Understand that innovation doesn't always mean inventions or radical departures from your way of doing things. It also encompasses gradual improvements in market approaches, processes and products.

4. Invest

Growth is often tied to the resources invested in a business. So, it's not surprising that managers tend to focus on increasing production capacity by investing in facility expansions or new equipment and technology.

In my opinion, getting the maximum benefit from your growth investments requires the following:

- Carrying out in-depth research on what's available in the marketplace before you make a major investment.

- When investing in technology, opt for turnkey solutions. Custom-made solutions are usually more expensive in the long run and lead to a degree of dependence on the supplier.

- Minimize the impact of the purchase on your cash flow by using business loans to finance your growth investments. Choose loans with repayment terms that match the asset's expected term of service.

Hang on to your money

There are a few simple ways to hang on to keep the money you make:

- Budget with savings in mind. There are many good budgeting tools out there. Pick one and use it.

- Record your expenses so that you can figure out how much you spend, then find ways you can cut that spending.

- Determine what you can put aside each week or month, then make saving successful by having money consistently and automatically transferred from your working account to your savings vehicle.

Enjoy life

This is simple but hard. Your money is a means to an end, nothing more and nothing less. If your end is to enjoy the good life—including your family, build that into your days right now. You have a limited number of minutes on this earth, and once a moment is gone, you never get it back.

Notes

_____

_____

_____

_____

_____

_____

_____

_____

_____

_____

_____

_____

CHAPTER 8

Questionnaire

The way to develop decisiveness is to start right where you are, with the very next question you face.

–Napoleon Hill

1. Am I ready to take the next step in growing my investments?

_____

_____

2. Do I have the availability and resources to proceed?

_____

_____

3. When do I want to take this step?

_____

_____

4. Why do I want to invest in the United States of America?

_____

_____

5. If this is for residency, what kind of visa will I pursue?

_____

_____

6. If this is for income, what type of entity will I form?

_____

_____

7. Do I feel comfortable with the analysis and due diligence I've performed?

_____

_____

8. Do I feel comfortable with the alternatives I've evaluated?

_____

_____

9. How and where will I find alliances and partners?

_____

_____

10. Will I invest 100 percent of my capital, or will I get bank loans?

_____

_____

11. Do I have the right banking relationships, lawyers and accountants?

_____

_____

12. Will I diversify my portfolio?

_____

_____

Notes

SUMMARY

Winning: The Art of Becoming an American Investor should have given you a solid grasp of what you'll need to do to become a successful investor and citizen in the United States.

Have you defined the purpose of the investment you're considering? What does your plan consist of, and have you taken any definitive action yet? For example, what kind of visa do you need, and how are you going to acquire it?

There are many company structures; which one do you feel most comfortable investing in? Have you created your team? Does it include an estate planning professional? What alliances have you managed to take advantage of?

Did you actually target a company and do a detailed analysis using the tools provided for you in this book? What about the case studies: did they help you with your analysis?

Do you understand how to accomplish the transition from your country to the United States? Are you cognizant of US taxation, banking forms and due diligence? Did you fill out the questionnaire at the end of the book, and are you ready for action?

If so, all the power to you; go forth and begin your journey to becoming a successful foreign investor in the United States of America.

bookofinvesting@gmail.com

Notes

_____

_____

_____

_____

_____

_____

_____

_____

_____

_____

_____

_____

ABOUT THE AUTHOR

Alejandro Dabdoub Smutny was born in Mexico City in 1972, the middle child of five siblings.

He has always enjoyed photography as an art, but his passion is for business, dealing with people, networking and creating new ventures.

Alejandro finished business administration at the University of New Orleans, took the real estate development program at Harvard executive education, completed an AD2 program at the IPADE Business School in Mexico City and studied infrastructure finance at the London Business School.

He started learning about corporate management in his grandfather's business, which his father sold. Since then, Alejandro has become an entrepreneur who builds restaurants—one of which is listed in the top 10 best restaurants in Mexico City. Given that the restaurant just mentioned had great wine sales, he became a wine distributor and eventually opened a number of retail shops.

On the artistic side, Alejandro has published two books of photography and was the producer of four different movies, one of which was invited to the Cannes festival and won a prize at the Paris film festival.

His main line of entrepreneurship, however, has always been in the development and construction of retail buildings and apartments. Alejandro began this line of business in 2001, where he developed his first shopping strip in Houston Texas and also started investing in apartment buildings with one of the most prestigious groups in the country. Since then, he has become (on invitation) a partner of the group and has participated in building a fund for international investors so they can invest in real estate in the United States.

Alejandro is also a partner in a real estate group in Mexico that develops high end condominiums as well as mixed use retail buildings. The group also developed a fund to integrate different construction companies in different states, allowing for the diversification of portfolios for its investors.

On the fun side, Alejandro collaborated with one of his partners to bring the sport of drifting to Mexico. This happened in 2008 and was the first drifting competition in Mexico. Today, he and his partner are building a drifting academy in Houston Texas, so they can eventually bring this kind of racing to that great state.

Alejandro is also part of a foundation that purchases art and lends it to museums around the world, so people can enjoy the beauty life has to offer.

Please visit Alejandro's website at
BecomingAnAmericanInvestor.com

www.ingramcontent.com/pod-product-compliance
Lightning Source LLC
Chambersburg PA
CBHW071204200326
41519CB00018B/5365